BACKYARD SCIENTIST

BACKYARD
PHYSICS
EXPERIMENTS

Alix Wood

PowerKiDS press

New York

Published in 2019 by Rosen Publishing
29 East 21st Street, New York, NY 10010

Produced for Rosen Publishing by Alix Wood Books
Designed by Alix Wood
Editor: Eloise Macgregor
Projects devised and photographed by Kevin Wood

Photo credits:
Cover, 1, 4, 6 top, 7 top © Adobe Stock Images;
all other photos © Kevin Wood

Cataloging-in-Publication Data
Names: Wood, Alix.
Title: Backyard physics experiments / Alix Wood.
Description: New York : PowerKids Press, 2019. | Series: Backyard scientist | Includes glossary and
index.
Identifiers: LCCN ISBN 9781538337462 (pbk.) | ISBN 9781538337455 (library bound) |
ISBN 9781538337479 (6 pack)
Subjects: LCSH: Physics--Experiments--Juvenile literature. | Science--Experiments--Juvenile
literature.
Classification: LCC QC26.W64 2019 | DDC 530.078--dc23

Printed in the United States of America

CPSIA compliance information: Batch # CS18PK: For further information contact Rosen Publishing, New York, New York at 1-800-237-9932.

Contents

What Is Physics?..4

Explore Gravity...6

The Egg Challenge..8

Gravity-Defying Kite...10

Snake Charming...12

Make a Water Wheel...14

Lemon Power!...16

Rocket Launch..18

Tennis Ball Cannon...20

Good Vibrations..22

Make a Paper Chair...24

Centrifugal Force..26

Test Your Physics Know-How...28

Glossary...30

For More Information...31

Index..32

What Is Physics?

Physics is a branch of science that studies how objects, **forces**, and energy all **interact**. A force is the push or pull on an object that may cause the object to speed up, slow down, stay in one place, or change shape. Energy is how things change and move. There are many different kinds of energy. Electricity and heat are both examples of types of energy. Scientists who work with physics are called physicists.

All About Forces

Back in the 1600s, scientist Isaac Newton watched an apple fall from a tree. He realized that a force, **gravity**, pulled things toward Earth. Newton was interested in what made things move. He discovered that when you push or pull an object, you are exerting a force on it. As long as the object is not held by something, the harder you push or pull, the faster the object will move. His work formed the basis of the science of physics.

Setting Up Your Backyard Laboratory

Find an outside space that you can use to do these experiments. Some of them are pretty messy! Remember to check with whomever owns the space that it is OK to do your experiments there. You may want to find a picnic table to work on.

You should be able to find most of the things you will need around your home or yard. You may need to buy some small items, so check the "You Will Need" section before you start a project.

BE SCIENTIFIC

As a scientist you will conduct experiments. An experiment is a test done in order to learn something or to discover if something works or is true.

Ask yourself a question you want to answer, such as "Do all apples fall at the same speed?" Then think of an experiment you can do that might answer your question.

STAYING SAFE

Science experiments can be dangerous. The experiments in this book have been specially chosen because they are fun and relatively safe, but you must still be careful. Ask an adult to help you. Follow all warnings. Wear any suggested protective clothing, and be careful.

Explore Gravity

Gravity is the force that pulls things toward the center of Earth. **Friction** is a force that can cause that fall to slow down. Try these experiments to find out how gravity and friction work.

1

Pour 1 inch (2.5 cm) of flour into a bowl. Ask someone to drop both balls into the flour at exactly the same time. Can you predict which ball will hit the flour first?

2

Was your prediction right? Try it a few more times to be sure of your result.

3

4

Place the bowl of flour at the bottom of your ramp. Roll both balls down the ramp at the same time. Try changing the angle of the ramp. Do both balls arrive together or does one take longer?

What happens when you roll the balls down a ramp? Make a ramp using some wood and a step or a flowerpot.

WHAT'S HAPPENING?

Gravity makes everything fall at the same rate, no matter how heavy it is. When you roll things down a ramp, another force is at work, too, known as friction. Friction is when one object rubs against another. It causes the balls to slow down. Why do you think the tennis ball was slower?

The Egg Challenge

What would happen if you dropped an egg from an upstairs window? You can be pretty sure the egg would smash. One way to slow down the force of gravity is by using **air resistance**. Try building an egg parachute and see if you can keep your egg from breaking.

1 Cut the largest square you can from one side of a big trash bag. Cut four pieces of string, each the length of one side of your square.

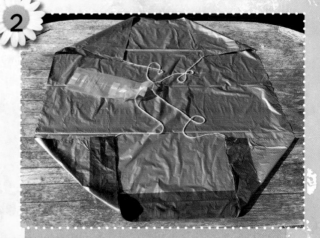

2 Tape one end of each piece of string to each corner. Tie the other end of each string to the sandwich bag handles.

3

Carefully place an egg into the sandwich bag.

4

Ask an adult to drop your egg parachute out of an upstairs window. Did the egg break?

WHAT'S HAPPENING?

As the parachute opens, its large surface area creates air resistance, which slows down the egg's fall. Try using a smaller bag. Did your egg fall faster? Did it break?

Gravity-Defying Kite

A parachute can slow down a falling object. A kite can actually go against gravity and travel up in the air. How? Kites are shaped and angled so air moving over the top moves faster than air moving over the bottom. This creates an upward force known as **lift**. Build your own kite and see this force in action.

YOU WILL NEED:

- large plastic trash bag
- small plastic bag
- a ball of string
- 2 sticks
- tape
- scissors

ADULT HELP NEEDED

1 Cut a large diamond shape out of the plastic trash bag, like in the photo above. Folding the bag in half may help you get the sides even.

2 Lay two sticks in a T-shape to make the frame for your kite. Ask an adult to cut the sticks to fit. Tape the ends of the sticks to the kite's corners.

3 Tape the sticks together where they cross at the center.

4 Cut the small bag into strips and tape them together. Then tape this long strip to the bottom corner of your kite.

5 Cut a length of string longer than the width of the kite. Tie it to each end of the horizontal stick. Tie the end of the ball of string to the center of this horizontal string.

IMPORTANT! NEVER fly a kite near power cables. It is dangerous.

WHAT'S HAPPENING?

To fly your kite, let out some string and run toward the direction the wind is coming from. The air movement will lift the kite into the sky. The tail helps balance the kite.

11

Snake Charming

Have you ever taken off a wool sweater and noticed that your hair stands on end? This is caused by **static electricity**. Static electricity occurs when a buildup of **electrons** give something an electric charge. Try this experiment, and try to charm a tissue paper snake using static electricity.

1

Place the tissue paper over the snake template (right). Trace the shape using a pencil, as marker may seep through your paper and ruin this book.

2

Cut out your snake. You may want an adult to help you. Decorate it using markers.

3

Rub a plastic ruler vigorously over the wool object for a few minutes.

WHAT'S HAPPENING?

Rubbing a plastic ruler against wool causes an **electrical charge** to be created. Charged electrons in the ruler are attracted to the tissue paper. Because the snake is so light, the static electricity can lift it.

4

Quickly hover the ruler over the snake. The snake will be attracted to the ruler, and start to rise up!

Make a Water Wheel

Energy created using the motion of water caused by gravity is known as **hydropower**. Hydropower is one of the oldest types of energy. Try building your own water wheel and use water power to lift a small weight.

YOU WILL NEED:

- two paper plates
- a stapler
- 7 paper cups
- a meat skewer
- some tape
- spool of thread
- PVA glue
- markers
- some water

ADULT HELP NEEDED

1

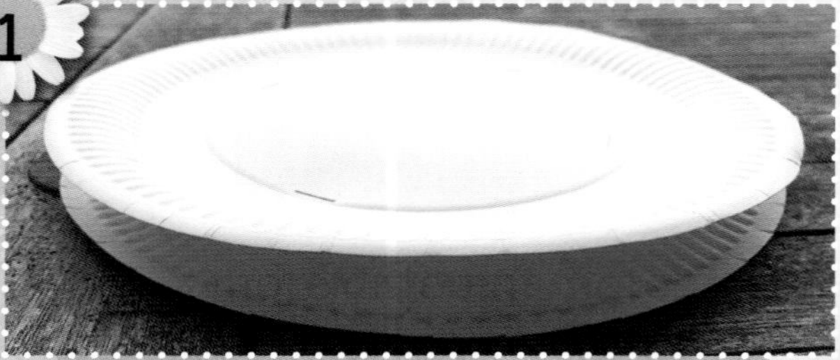

Staple two paper plates together, back to back.

2

Rest 6 paper cups in the groove between the two plates, and tape them in place. All the cups must face in the same direction. You can decorate your wheel using markers.

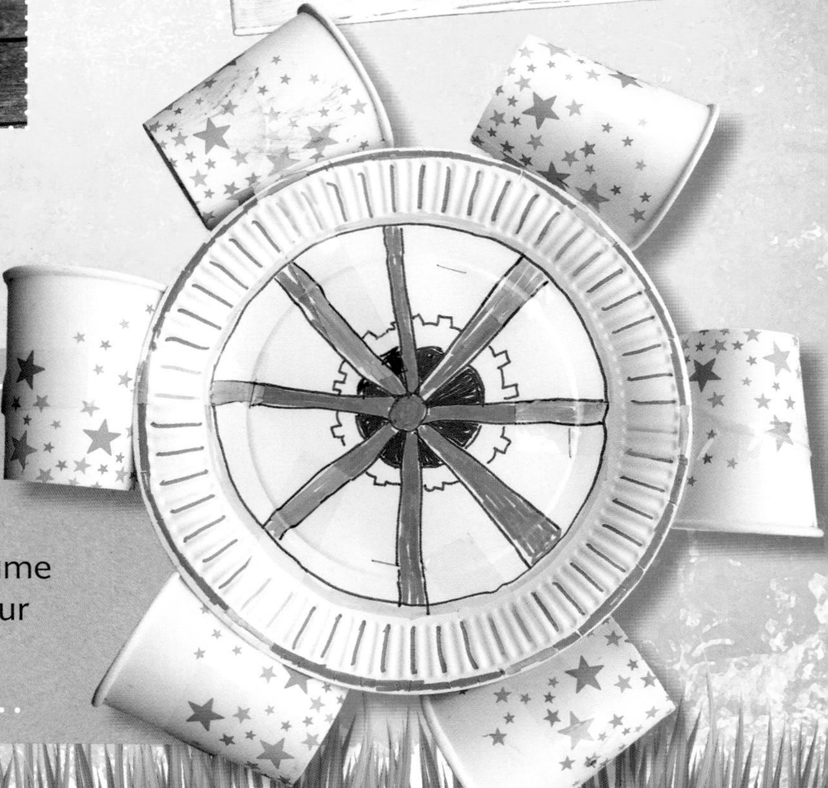

3

Glue a spool of thread to the center of your water wheel. Let it dry. Ask an adult to push a skewer through the spool and paper plate.

4

Tie the end of the thread to a small weight. We used another paper cup.

5

Hold the skewer. Pour water into a top cup to make the wheel spin.

WHAT'S HAPPENING?

Pouring water causes the water wheel to spin. This produces enough energy to turn the spool, and raise the weight.

Lemon Power!

Did you know you could make a battery out of a lemon? If you push something zinc and something copper into a lemon and connect the two metals, the lemon power created is enough to light an **LED**! You can get alligator clips and an LED from an electrical supply store.

1 Insert a copper penny or copper wire into a cut made on one side of a lemon. Push a zinc nail into the other side of the lemon. The nail and penny must not touch.

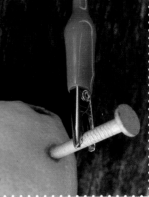

2 Connect the copper to the LED using one alligator clip wire. Connect the nail to the bulb using another alligator clip wire. The bulb may light up.

3

If your bulb didn't light up, you may need more lemon-power!

4

Link more lemons together in a chain by connecting each zinc nail to the next lemon's copper wire as shown. Connect each end of the chain to the bulb.

WHAT'S HAPPENING?

Batteries contain two metals in an acid **solution**. Our lemon battery works because lemons contain citric acid. When you connect the zinc nail and copper wire, in the lemon's acidic solution, a **current** will flow, just like in a battery. Connecting the lemon battery to a bulb completes the **circuit**. How many lemons did you need to light your bulb?

Rocket Launch

One of the laws of physics is that for every action, there is an equal and opposite reaction. In this experiment, see how the pressure of gas exploding from a bottle can launch it into the air! The action of the downward push by the gas creates an upward reaction in the opposite direction. This experiment can be dangerous. Do not approach the rocket once it is ready for liftoff.

YOU WILL NEED:

- large plastic bottle
- a cork that fits the bottle
- half a sheet of paper towel
- three pencils
- tape
- baking soda
- vinegar
- scissors

ADULT HELP NEEDED

1

Turn the bottle upside down. Tape three pencils to the sides. Level the pencils so the bottle stands up when you turn it over, and allow for space under the cork.

2

Put 1/2 tablespoon of baking soda in the center of half a sheet of paper towel. Roll the towel like a sausage and twist the ends closed.

3

Turn your bottle over.
Fill it halfway with vinegar.

WHAT'S HAPPENING?

The force that propels the rocket is caused by a **chemical reaction**. Mixing vinegar and baking soda creates **carbon dioxide** gas. Once the gas has filled the bottle, it blasts off the cork with great force, shooting the bottle into the air.

4

Ask an adult to drop the baking soda towel into the bottle, and quickly push in the cork.

5

Have the adult quickly turn the bottle over. Stand back. Do not approach the bottle if it does not go off. The reaction can take a while to work.

Tennis Ball Cannon

You can turn a tennis ball tube or potato chip can into a cannon. Try this experiment using **potential energy**. Potential energy is stored energy. You can use the power you have stored in a stretched rubber band to shoot a tennis ball out of your cannon.

YOU WILL NEED:

- tennis ball or potato chip can
- a plastic bottle that will fit in the can
- tennis ball
- scissors
- pencil or skewer
- 2 strong rubber bands

ADULT HELP NEEDED

1

Ask an adult to help cut the bottom from the tube. Make two slits near one end of the can about 1/2 inch (1.3 cm) apart. Do the same on the opposite side of the can.

2

Push a rubber band through the slits on each side of the can. Tie each rubber band in a knot to secure them.

3

Ask an adult to help you poke two holes on opposite sides of the bottle, at the point where the bottle starts to slope toward the lid. Push the pencil through the holes.

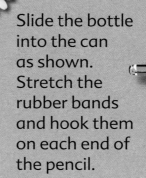

4

Slide the bottle into the can as shown. Stretch the rubber bands and hook them on each end of the pencil.

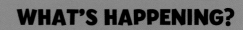

5

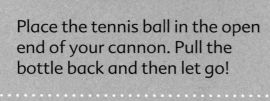

Place the tennis ball in the open end of your cannon. Pull the bottle back and then let go!

WHAT'S HAPPENING?

Pulling back on the rubber bands transfers energy from ourselves to the bands. Releasing the bands uses the stored energy to fire the ball.

Good Vibrations

Have you ever wondered what sounds are, and how we can hear them? When you clap your hands, you shake air **molecules** around your hands and cause them to vibrate. That vibration will spread from molecule to molecule, allowing the sound to travel. When air vibrations enter your ear, you are able to hear the sound because they vibrate the eardrum.

YOU WILL NEED:

- paper cup
- balloon
- a straw
- some tape
- scissors

1

Cut the bottom off the paper cup using scissors.

2

Cut the top off a balloon using scissors. You need enough balloon left to be able to stretch it over the bottom of your cup.

22

3

Stretch the balloon tightly over the bottom of the cup and tape it in place.

4

Cut the straw in half and put half into the end of the balloon. Tape the straw in place.

Blow into the straw.
You should make a sound like a horn!

WHAT'S HAPPENING?

Blowing into the straw causes the stretched balloon to vibrate and make a sound. The cup acts like a speaker, making the sound louder. If your horn doesn't work, check that your balloon is stretched tightly enough.

Make a Paper Chair

Do you think you could sit on a chair made of paper? Surprisingly, paper can hold the weight of a person, if you understand physics! Try this experiment and learn how columns can help spread a heavy load.

YOU WILL NEED:

- lots of newspaper, wallpaper, or comics
- some tape
- packing tape

1

Tightly roll some sheets of paper. With newspaper, roll a section of four pages, starting at the crease and rolling toward the edge. Secure the roll with tape. Add layers until the cylinder is about the size of a toilet paper tube.

2

Repeat step 1 to make more paper columns. The more columns you make, the stronger the chair will be. Tape three columns together in a line.

3

Tape two cylinders above and two below your three columns. You could probably already sit on this stool!

4

When you think you have enough columns, wrap packing tape around your stool. You could wrap comics or wallpaper around it. Paper isn't waterproof, so don't leave it out in the rain.

Try making a back for your chair.

WHAT'S HAPPENING?

One paper column would bend if you sat on it. However, joining several columns together means they share your weight. This is known as a **distributed load**. Your paper chair can support you because your weight is spread evenly between all the columns. Each column only has to support a percentage of your weight.

Centrifugal Force

When a car you are in takes a sharp left turn, your body can feel as if it is being pushed to the right. Why? Because objects want to travel in a straight line. As the turning car pulls you to the left, your body resists and tries to keep traveling forward! This effect is known as **centrifugal force**. Learn about it with this messy experiment.

1

Can you keep a ball in a swinging bucket? Try it.

2

Swing the bucket upside down. Try not to let the ball fall out.

3

Once you have your technique, put some water in the bucket and try it again.

4

If you keep up your speed, and keep a smooth motion, the water should stay in the bucket. If you slow down or move jerkily, the water may come out!

WHAT'S HAPPENING?

As the bucket swings, centrifugal force pushes the water away from the center and toward the bottom of the bucket. This keeps the water from spilling. If the swinging stopped, the water would spill, as the force of gravity would pull the water toward the center of the Earth.

Are you a physics genius? Test yourself with these questions. The answers are on page 29.

1. **What force did Isaac Newton realize existed when he watched an apple fall from a tree?**
    a) lift   b) gravity   c) friction

2. **What happens if you drop two balls of different weights at the same time?**
    a) they hit the ground at the same time
    b) the heavier ball hits the ground first
    c) the lighter ball hits the ground first

3. **What can slow down the effect of gravity?**
   a) air resistance   b) friction   c) both a and b

4. **A big parachute would slow a falling object more effectively than a small parachute.**
   a) true   b) false

5. **What two things did you need to connect together to make the lemon battery work?**
   a) something gold and something silver
   b) something zinc and something copper
   c) something copper and something silver

6. What is the force called that causes a kite to move upward?
a) down force b) gravity c) lift

7. What causes your hair to stand on end when you take off
a wool sweater?
a) static electricity b) gravity c) air resistance

8. What is hydropower?
a) a boat
b) energy created by wind
c) energy created by running water

9. What would be the best way to make one sheet of newspaper
move a tennis ball along a flat surface?
a) fold the sheet in half and waft the ball
b) touch the ball with the opened-out sheet of paper
c) roll the sheet tightly into a cylinder and hit the ball with it

10. What force helps keep water in a swinging bucket?
a) centrifugal force b) gravity c) friction

Answers

1. b) gravity; 2. a) they hit the ground at the same time; 3. c) both a
and b; 4. a) true; 5. b) something zinc and something copper;
6. c) lift; 7. a) static electricity; 8. c) energy created by running
water; 9. c) roll the sheet tightly into a cylinder and hit the ball with
it; 10. a) centrifugal force

Glossary

air resistance A frictional force air exerts on a moving object.

carbon dioxide A colorless gas.

centrifugal force An outward force on a body rotating about an axis.

chemical reaction A process in which atoms of the same or different elements rearrange themselves to form a new substance.

circuit The complete path of an electric current.

current A stream of electric charge.

distributed load A load that is shared evenly over a surface.

electrical charge An amount of electricity that is held or carried.

electrons Particles that have a negative charge of electricity.

forces Influences (such as a push or pull) that tend to produce a change in a subject's speed or direction of motion.

friction The force that resists motion between bodies in contact.

gravity A force of attraction between bodies due to their mass.

hydropower Power produced by the movement of water.

interact To act on one another.

LED A light-emitting diode.

lift An upward force.

molecules The smallest particles of a substance.

potential energy Stored energy.

solution A liquid in which something has been dissolved.

static electricity A stationary electric charge, typically produced by friction.

Brown, Jordan D. *Science Stunts: Fun Feats of Physics.* Watertown, MA: Imagine Publishing, 2016.

Jacoby, Jenny. *STEM Starters For Kids Physics Activity Book.* New York, NY: Skyhorse Publishing, 2018.

Mercer, Bobby. *Junk Drawer Physics: 50 Awesome Experiments That Don't Cost a Thing.* Chicago, IL: Chicago Review Press, 2014.

Parker, Steve. *Fizzing Physics: Fantastic Hands-on Activities.* London, UK: QEB Publishing, 2016.

Websites
Due to the changing nature of Internet links, PowerKids Press has developed an online list of websites related to the subject of this book. This site is updated regularly. Please use this link to access the list:

www.powerkidslinks.com/bs/physics

Index

air resistance 8, 9

batteries 16, 17
bulb 16, 17

carbon dioxide 19
centrifugal force 26, 27
circuit 17
columns 24, 25
copper 16, 17
current 17

distributed loads 24, 25

electrical charges 13
electricity 4, 12, 13
electrons 12, 13
energy 4, 14, 15, 20, 21

forces 4, 6, 7, 8, 10, 18, 19, 26, 27
friction 6, 7

gas 18, 19
gravity 4, 6, 7, 8, 9, 14

heat 4

hydropower 14

LED 16, 17
lift 10, 11

molecules 22

Newton, Sir Isaac 4

potential energy 20, 21
power 16, 17

reaction 18, 19

sound 22, 23
static electricity 12, 13

zinc 16, 17